E $7.45
Ar   Arvetis, Chris
         Why does it snow

DATE DUE

OC 31 '89	JY 11 '91	JY 14 '93	JAN 02 '97
NO 24 89	AG 8 '91	NOV 07 94	MAY 09 '97
DE 15 '89	AG 26 '91	NOV 23 94	JUL 09 '97
MR 19 '90	OC 5 '91	DEC 06 94	DEC 01 '97
JY 6 '90	NO 29 91	AUG 31 '95	FEB 04 '98
JY 23 '90	DE 21 '91	SEP 28 95	MR 01 '98
JY 28 '90	JY 11 '92	OCT 26 95	MAY 01 '98
AG 9 '90	JA 1 '93	JAN 17 96	JUL 10 '98
SE 4 '90	JA 28 '93	MAR 18 96	L 27 '98
OC 5 '90	FE 13 '93	APR 20 96	6 20 '98
AP 16 '91	JE 10 '93	NOV 07 96	JN 22
JE 28 91			JY 08 '00

Why Does It Snow?

A **Just Ask** Book

Hi, my name is Christopher!

by Chris Arvetis
and Carole Palmer

illustrated by James Buckley

Copyright © 1986 by Rand McNally & Company
All rights reserved
Printed in Italy

Library of Congress Catalog Card Number: 85-63023

EAU CLAIRE DISTRICT LIBRARY

CHILDRENS PRESS CHOICE

A Rand McNally title selected for educational distribution

ISBN 0-516-09810-1

1986 SCHOOL AND LIBRARY EDITION

Christopher!
Come on out.
It's snowing!
We're all here
to play.

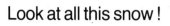
Look at all this snow !

Okay, Okay.
I see the snow!
But before we play
I want to find out–
why does it snow?

I have no idea.

I don't either, but we could ask someone !

Can you tell us—
why does it snow?

I think I can.
Come into the house.
I'll show you a picture
to explain.

This is a cloud.
It is high up in the
sky where it is very,
very cold.

The cloud is made up of tiny ice crystals and tiny drops of water.

As the tiny drops of water become very, very cold, the drops stick to the ice crystals and freeze.
It's nice and warm in here !

Then the ice crystals get bigger and bigger.
We call them snowflakes.
As the snowflakes get bigger they get heavy, too.
Then they fall from the clouds.

If the air below the cloud is warm, the snowflakes turn into water and become rain. If the air is cold, the snowflakes fall to the ground and it snows.

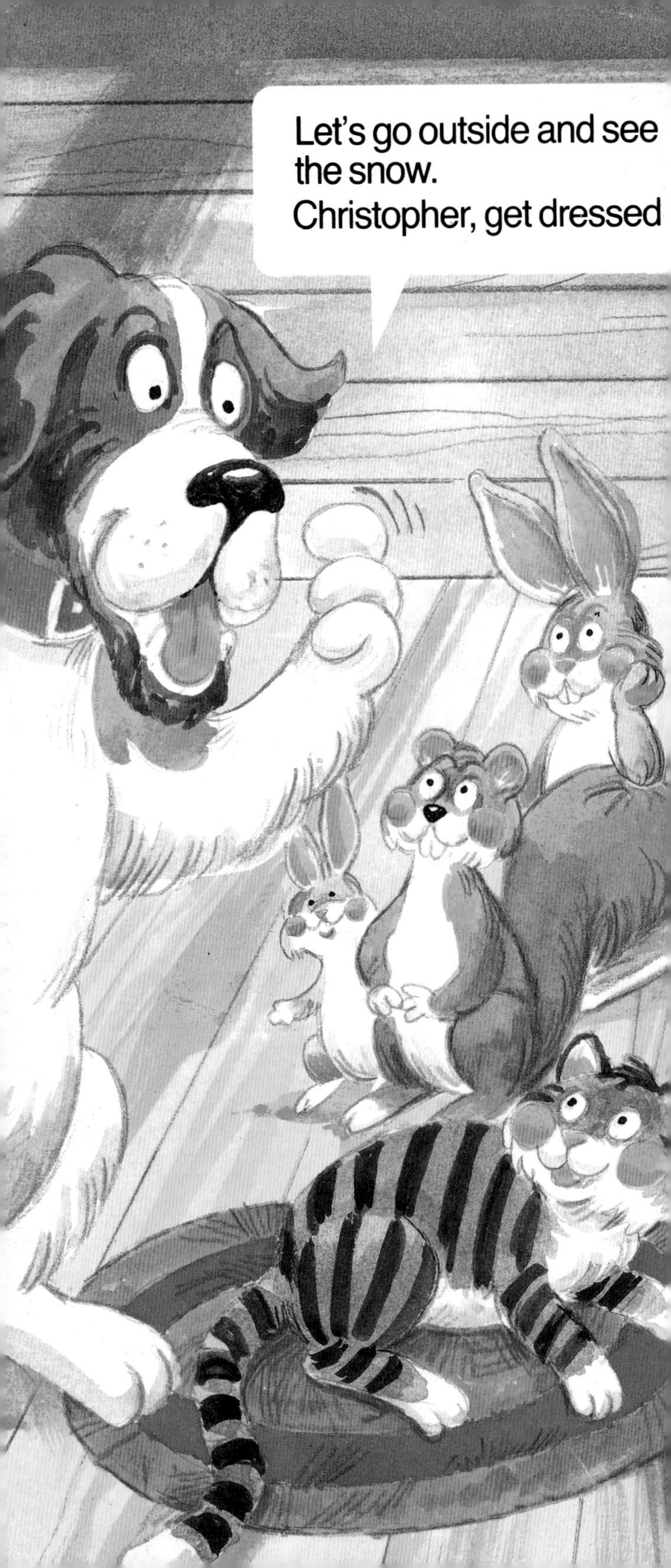
Let's go outside and see the snow.
Christopher, get dressed

Look at the snowflakes.
Each one has six sides.
Some look like stars.
No two snowflakes are
ever exactly alike.
Look how pretty they are.

Sometimes it is very cold
and windy when it snows.
A lot of snow falls.
Then we have a *snowstorm*.
When the wind blows the
snow into large piles, we
have *snowdrifts*.

In big snowstorms, we use
snow shovels and *snowplows*
to clear the roads and paths.

Sometimes we use *snowshoes*
to walk over the snow.

Others use *skis*.

Still others ride on *sleds*
and *snowmobiles*.

And we can have fun in the snow by making large *snowballs* to make a *snowman*.

Just remember—
when the drops of water in
the clouds freeze and fall
to the ground, it snows.

Then we see—
snowflakes, snowstorms,
snowdrifts, snowplows,
and snowsuits.

And maybe even snowshoes,
snowmobiles, and a snowman.

And now I know
why it snows!